TOOLS FOR CAREGIVERS

- **F&P LEVEL:** B
- **WORD COUNT:** 25
- **CURRICULUM CONNECTIONS:** animals, habitats, nature

Skills to Teach

- **HIGH-FREQUENCY WORDS:** a, has, in, is, it, on
- **CONTENT WORDS:** brown, claws, climbs, eats, fur, hangs, holds, sleeps, sloth, tree
- **PUNCTUATION:** periods
- **WORD STUDY:** /k/, spelled c (claws, climbs); long /e/, spelled ea (eats); long /e/, spelled ee (sleeps, tree)
- **TEXT TYPE:** information report

Before Reading Activities

- Read the title and give a simple statement of the main idea.
- Have students "walk" through the book and talk about what they see in the pictures.
- Introduce new vocabulary by having students predict the first letter and locate the word in the text.
- Discuss any unfamiliar concepts that are in the text.

After Reading Activities

Have readers flip back through the book. What do they see the sloths in the book doing? What do sloths do in trees? What body parts help a sloth live in the trees? Ask readers to point to each example in the book.

Tadpole Books are published by Jump!, 5357 Penn Avenue South, Minneapolis, MN 55419, www.jumplibrary.com

Copyright ©2024 Jump. International copyright reserved in all countries. No part of this book may be reproduced in any form without written permission from the publisher.

Editor: Jenna Gleisner **Designer:** Emma Almgren-Bersie

Photo Credits: Joel Sartore/Photo Ark/Nature Picture Library, cover; Eric Isselee/Shutterstock, 1; Damsea/Shutterstock, 2tl, 2tr, 6–7; Oyvind Martinsen-Panama Wildlife/Alamy, 2ml, 10–11; Jenhuang99/Dreamstime, 2mr, 4–5; KenCanning/iStock, 2bl, 8–9, 12–13; Josanel Sugasti/Shutterstock, 2br, 14–15; Rob Jansen/Shutterstock, 3; Clara Bastian/Shutterstock, 16tl; Vaclav Matous/Shutterstock, 16tr; Ondrej Prosicky/Shutterstock, 16bl; Jsegalexplore/Shutterstock, 16br.

Library of Congress Cataloging-in-Publication Data
Names: Brandle, Marie, 1989– author.
Title: Sloths / by Marie Brandle.
Description: Minneapolis, MN: Jump!, Inc., (2024)
Series: My first animal books | Includes index.
Audience: Ages 3–6
Identifiers: LCCN 2022054086 (print)
LCCN 2022054087 (ebook)
ISBN 9798885246828 (hardcover)
ISBN 9798885246835 (paperback)
ISBN 9798885246842 (ebook)
Subjects: LCSH: Sloths—Juvenile literature.
Classification: LCC QL737.E2 B73 2024 (print)
LCC QL737.E2 (ebook)
DDC 599.3/13—dc23/eng/20221110
LC record available at https://lccn.loc.gov/2022054086
LC ebook record available at https://lccn.loc.gov/2022054087
LC ebook record available at https://lccn.loc.gov/2022054045

MY FIRST ANIMAL BOOKS

SLOTHS

by Marie Brandle

TABLE OF CONTENTS

Words to Know.............................2

Sloths....................................3

Let's Review!...........................16

Index..................................16

WORDS TO KNOW

claws

climbs

eats

fur

hangs

sleeps

SLOTHS

A sloth is in a tree.

It has brown fur.

It has claws.

It climbs.

leaf

It eats.

baby sloth

It holds on.

It sleeps.

LET'S REVIEW!

Sloths climb trees. Point to the other animals below that climb trees.

INDEX

claws 6
climbs 7
eats 11
fur 5

hangs 9
sleeps 15
tree 3